Helen Exley Giftbooks
for the most thoughtful gifts of all

OTHER BOOKS IN THIS SERIES:
For a wonderful Mother A book to make your own
For a wonderful Grandmother A book to make your own
For a real Friend A book to make your own
A Girl's Journal A personal notebook and keepsake
A Woman's Journal A personal notebook and keepsake
Cats A book to make your own
Inspirations A book to make your own
A Gardener's Journal A book to make your own
OTHER HELEN EXLEY GIFTBOOKS
ON TEDDY BEARS:
Teddy Bear Quotations
The Littlest Teddy Bear Book
Teddy Lovers Address Book

Published in hardback 1990. Published in softcover 2001.
Copyright © Helen Exley 1990, 2001
Selection © Helen Exley 1990, 2001
The moral right of the author has been asserted.

12 11 10 9 8 7 6 5 4 3 2 1

ISBN 1-86187-218-6

Selection and design by Helen Exley
Illustrated by Juliette Clarke
Printed in China

Exley Publications Ltd, 16 Chalk Hill, Watford, Herts, WD1 4BN, UK.
Exley Publications LLC, 232 Madison Avenue, Suite 1409, NY 10016, USA.
Acknowledgements: The publishers are grateful for permission to reproduce copyright material. Whilst every reasonable effort has been made to trace copyright holders, we would be pleased to hear from any not here acknowledged. Peter Bull: From *A Hug of Teddy Bears* published by The Herbert Press/A&C Black; From *The Teddy Bear Book* published by Hobby House Press Inc. Gill Davies: Used by permission of the author © 1995 Gill Davies. Ted Menten: From *The Teddy Bear Lover's Companion* published by Courage Books, an imprint of Running Press © 1991. Used by permission. Gustav Severin: From *Teddy Bear* published by Transedition Books/Andromeda Oxford Ltd. 1994.

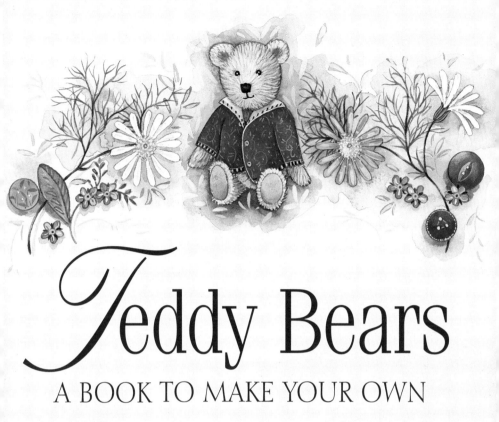

Teddy Bears

A BOOK TO MAKE YOUR OWN

A HELEN EXLEY GIFTBOOK

EXLEY
NEW YORK • WATFORD, UK

..."*Happy*" *seems to epitomize the sheer beauty*
and character we all seek in our teddy bears —
gaze into those great big eyes and your heart just melts!

MARGARET AND GERRY GREY, FROM "TEDDY BEARS"

A TEDDY IS A CUDDLE WITH FOUR PAWS ON·THE END.

GILL DAVIES

*With their fur rubbed bald from loving hands,
their ears resewn or replaced, their paw pads frayed and patched
[teddy bears] make me feel like a child again,
seeking love, understanding, and security from a hostile
and frightening adult world.*

TED MENTEN,
FROM "THE TEDDY BEAR LOVER'S COMPANION"

*W*ise teachers – well kind ones, anyway –
invite teddies to school on the very first day.

JAMES FURY

Am I alone in finding a row of Teddy Bears
set up for sale at auction a sad sight?
They are like lost pets....
They are toys that have lost their children,
toys that recall childhood past and finished.

MARY HILLIER

Some parents make the hideous error of getting rid of an old,
battered and possibly smelly but beloved bear and substituting
a brand new extremely expensive one. A child of four could tell them
this is nothing short of criminal.

PETER BULL (1912-1984),
FROM "A HUG OF TEDDY BEARS"

$\mathcal{T}$he secret, in my opinion,
of the continued appeal of the Teddy
is his immense ability to listen
and understand.

PETER BULL (1912-1984),
FROM "BEST OF TEDDY BEAR
AND FRIENDS"

They have all grown and gone...
outwardly changed beyond belief.
But Bear sits on the chest of drawers,
just as he always has,
and holds their childhood safe,
until they need him once again.

HELEN THOMSON, B.1943

$\mathcal{D}$id you know that the teddy has been called
the world's most popular soft toy?
That in Britain, 63 houses out of every 100
have one? That there are more than 140 million
of them in the U.S.A.?

LEO ZANELLI

I think about the times during my travels
that I've awakened in the night in some strange hotel room,
disoriented until I recognize one of my bears
sitting nearby, like a sentry. It doesn't matter where I am;
if there are teddies nearby, I know that I am safe.

TED MENTEN,
FROM "THE TEDDY BEAR LOVER'S COMPANION"

He [a teddy bear]
is a constant link in a chain of love,
his position and status similar
to that of a pagan household god,
protecting successive generations.

GENEVIÈVE AND GÉRARD PICOT

Any bear knows more about listening
than any psychiatrist.

MAYA V. PATEL, B.1943

The world of the teddy bear
is an innocent one,
a world that
"gives delight and hurts not",
a world that appeals
to all generations
and all nationalities.

GYLES BRANDRETH

Teddy Bears shouldn't sit in closets
when there's a child around who will love them.

JANET DAILEY, B.1944

THROUGH THE HARD TIMES...

What a miracle life is, and how whimsical
that in all their wonder and their pain,
their confusion and their joy, human beings
had the idea to create teddy bears
to keep them company and help
them make it through the hard times.

TED MENTEN,
FROM "THE TEDDY BEAR LOVER'S COMPANION"

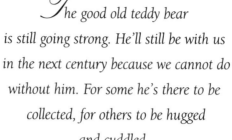

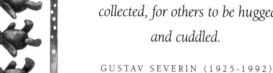

The good old teddy bear is still going strong. He'll still be with us in the next century because we cannot do without him. For some he's there to be collected, for others to be hugged and cuddled.

GUSTAV SEVERIN (1925-1992)

A teddy bear can become the object of
any kind of love by any kind of person.
Out of a choice of hundreds
or even thousands of teddies each person
can find just the right bear to love.

HELEN THOMSON, B.1943

At some point the day arrives when the child, now a grownup,
starts rummaging around for the memories of their youth in general
and for their old teddy in particular.
The reunion awakens deeply slumbering emotions
and the bear, this leftover from an untroubled childhood,
is elevated to a place of honor....

GUSTAV SEVERIN (1925-1992), FROM "TEDDY BEAR"

EVERY IMMACULATE HOME

NEEDS A DILAPIDATED BEAR SITTING AROUND SOMEWHERE –

JUST TO REMIND YOU THAT A HOME IS FOR LIVING IN.

B.R. MEADOWS

... he (or she) can enter a secret world with Teddy.
No demands, no regulations and, above all,
a sympathetic and understanding friend
to have constantly at one's elbow.

PETER BULL (1912-1984),
FROM "A HUG OF TEDDY BEARS"

MINE

He may not be as beautiful as lots of Teds you see

He isn't new with ribbons or as big as big can be

He's small and old and tired with a bandage round his knee

But he's really truly special

'Cos he all belongs to me.

GILL DAVIES

$\mathscr{A}$ll bears merit a Dignified Old Age.

PETER GRAY

Bears have life breathed into them by years of loving

MARION C. GARRETTY, B.1917

A teddy is a friend
who is always waiting there
Soft and warm and smiling
a cuddly snuggly bear
Some people are like teddies
And one of them is you
You're snuggly, warm and comfy
but can I keep my teddy too?

GILL DAVIES

*Looking into the eyes of the Most-Loved Teddy Bear contenders,
I am smitten.... I give each tousled bear the definitive test – a hug.
And the prize goes to that very special teddy bear that makes
me feel most loved.*

TED   MENTEN

A teddy bear appears to children as a kind of guardian angel in a shaggy coat and they won't do without its cuddly presence even when they are asleep. Nor does it bother them when their bear loses its hair and becomes unpresentable; quite the opposite: worn-off fur, patches, and other signs of age only serve to increase its charm and strengthen the inner bonds.

GUSTAV SEVERIN (1925-1992),
FROM "TEDDY BEAR"

A bear does not go in for brains
and hearts and bones and such.
He hasn't room for them.
He is packed tight with love.

PAM BROWN, B.1928

There is something remarkable
about teddy bears.
It has been my experience
that I might have found myself grumpy –
but then I simply chance to look at a bear
and something happens.
My mood changes,
the furrowed brow disappears....

NANCI VAN ROOZENDAAL,
FROM "TEDDY BEARS PAST AND PRESENT"

You <u>know</u> his eyes are coloured glass.
Then why does he look so desperately disconsolate
when you go out and leave him behind?

PAM BROWN, B.1928

*... the teddy bear was born out of an act of kindness,
nurtured by an artist's gentle wit, and fashioned
by a physically handicapped toymaker to please
her beloved nephew. Right from the start,
the teddy bear represented the brightest side
of human nature.*

TED MENTEN,
FROM "THE TEDDY BEAR LOVER'S COMPANION"

An advantage of a Teddy as a friend
is that he will shoulder the blame for some misdemeanour
committed by his owner. "It wasn't me," you will hear
the child shout, "it was Teddy. Naughty, naughty Teddy!"
... Later, with luck, you will see the child apologizing
to his friend and asking for forgiveness,
which is readily given.

PETER BULL (1912-1984),
FROM "A HUG OF TEDDY BEARS"

LONG BEFORE I GREW UP,
MY TEDDY-BEAR TAUGHT ME WHAT LOVE REALLY MEANT –
BEING THERE WHEN YOU'RE NEEDED.

JIM NELSON

... does maturity mean abandoning our beloved teddy bears,

and truest childhood friends, or does it mean

being strong enough to proudly proclaim our devotion to them?

If I had to choose, there would be no contest –

the kind of maturity that has no room for whimsy

is meaningless and offers no reward.

Give me the warmth of a tattered teddy any day.

TED MENTEN,
FROM "THE TEDDY BEAR LOVER'S COMPANION"

IT TAKES A LOT OF LOVING
TO TURN A SHOP BEAR INTO A FRIEND.

PAM BROWN, B.1928

There's no such thing as a bad bear.
There are ugly bears and poorly made bears,
but each is capable of bringing a smile to someone's face,
a sense of fun or comfort.

MAC POHLEN, B.1950

... bears are sought by young and old alike
just to hug.
They have to be soft, snuggly, and indestructible.

GUSTAV SEVERIN (1925-1992),
FROM "TEDDY BEAR"

$\mathcal{S}$ometimes a friend can let you down,
sometimes a friend can talk too much
when you want to go to ground.
Sometimes it's just easier
to be in the same room as your old Teddy.

HELEN THOMSON, B.1943

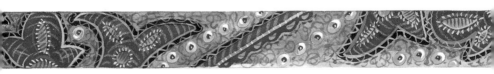

It's hard to visualize the toys
you had fifty years ago – all save bear.
He's as clear as if he were sitting
on the desk in front of you.
... of course... he probably is.

PAM BROWN, B.1928